Date Due			
2-18-76			
2-25-16			
4-7-76			
10-21			
9-28-78			

628
S

Showers, Paul
Where does the garbage go?

WHERE DOES THE GARBAGE GO ?

WHERE DOES THE GARBAGE GO ?

by **PAUL SHOWERS** **Illustrated by Loretta Lustig**

THOMAS Y. CROWELL COMPANY · NEW YORK

LET'S-READ-AND-FIND-OUT SCIENCE BOOKS

Editors: *DR. ROMA GANS*, Professor Emeritus of Childhood Education, Teachers College, Columbia University
DR. FRANKLYN M. BRANLEY, Astronomer Emeritus and former Chairman of The American Museum-Hayden Planetarium

Copyright © 1974 by Paul Showers. Illustrations copyright © 1974 by Loretta Lustig

Library of Congress Cataloging in Publication Data   Showers, Paul.   Where does the garbage go? (Let's read-and-find-out science book) SUMMARY: Discusses the growing garbage and trash problem in the United States and its possible solutions.   1. Refuse and refuse disposal—Juv. lit.   [1. Refuse and refuse disposal]   I. Lustig, Loretta, illus.   II. Title.   TD792.S48   628 .44   73-14881 ISBN 0-690-00392-7   ISBN 0-690-00402-8 (lib. bdg.)

WHERE DOES THE GARBAGE GO?

LET'S
READ
AND
FIND
OUT →

Everything goes in the garbage pail in our house. We throw in potato peelings, orange skins, bones, the food we don't eat, empty bottles and tin cans, plastic bags, paper, aluminum foil—all kinds of junk.

What goes into the garbage in your house?

Yesterday I dumped my wastebasket into the garbage pail. I dumped in pieces of cardboard, a broken pencil, my worn-out sneakers, an old shoebox, three buttons, and an old yo-yo. What do you put in the wastebasket? What does your father put in it?

My uncle and aunt live on a farm. The garbage is different at their house. Everything doesn't go into the garbage pail. In the kitchen there is a big bucket for garbage. A big box is in the corner for trash.

When I am at the farm, I scrape the plates into the garbage bucket. My aunt throws in other things—potato peelings, eggshells, apple cores, cabbage leaves, carrot tops, stale bread.

One day I threw in a broken cup. "Not there," my aunt said. "The garbage is for the pigs. Put the cup in the trash."

The trash box holds tin cans, bottles, old light bulbs, cracked cups, broken plates—all kinds of junk that pigs cannot eat.

When the box is full, my uncle takes it out behind the barn. He has a big hole there. He throws in the trash. He covers it with dirt. Another day he throws in more trash and more dirt. When the hole is filled up, my uncle digs another. My uncle has to dig a lot of holes.

Every day when I am at the farm, I carry the garbage bucket out to the pigs. I like to feed the pigs. They have blue eyes and big ears.

The garbage is their dessert. First they eat their regular dinner—corn, oats, milk, special foods. Then I dump the garbage into their feeding trough. They LOVE it. It is like ice cream to them. They chew with their mouths open—closh, closh, closh. It's fun to watch them.

Everywhere people live they make garbage and trash. In the United States they make a billion pounds a day. But nobody wants garbage and trash. Everybody wants to get rid of it.

Where I live we put the garbage pails out at the curb. A big white truck comes by. Men empty the pails into the back of the truck. Everything is pushed inside the truck.

Some apartment buildings have garbage chutes. You pull down a little door and dump in your trash and garbage. It all falls down the chute to the basement. In the basement there is an incinerator. It is a special furnace that burns garbage and trash.

Some people use compacters. A compacter squeezes garbage, bottles, and cans into a small, tight lump. This takes up less room in the garbage pail.

Some people have a garbage grinder in the sink. It grinds up the garbage so it can run down the drain.

How do you get rid of the garbage at your house?

There is one big trouble about garbage. People never really get rid of it. They just move it away from their houses to some other place.

Many cities used to dump their garbage in rivers or lakes. New York City threw its garbage into the ocean. It put the garbage on flat boats called barges. Tugboats pulled the barges out to sea. The garbage was dumped overboard into the water. Sometimes the water carried the garbage back to the land. It floated to beaches where people were swimming. Ughhh! Yeccch!

New York and the other cities had to stop dumping garbage into the ocean or the lakes and rivers near them.

Now many cities burn their garbage in big incinerators. But even that doesn't get rid of all of it. When garbage burns, it makes smoke and ashes. The smoke goes up the chimney. It makes the air we breathe dirty. The ashes are left in the incinerator. They have to be taken away in trucks.

17

Today many cities still send their garbage to the dump. A city dump is a dirty place. It is a great big mess covered with junk — worn-out tires, piles of garbage, broken chairs, cardboard boxes, plastic bags, old newspapers, millions of tin cans, billions of pieces of broken glass — all the things no one wants anymore.

All day the trucks come from the city. They
follow little roads across the junk. At the end of
the road they dump their loads. In summer the
garbage rots and stinks. Rats come to eat it.
Millions of flies buzz around.

Cities are supposed to cover up their junk and garbage, the same way my uncle does on the farm. City dumps use bulldozers to dig holes and scoop up dirt. The bulldozers spread dirt over the piles of junk. That helps to keep away rats and flies. The dirt keeps the garbage from stinking too much.

Do you know where the trucks take the garbage in your city? Does your city have a dump? Did you ever see it? What did it look like? Every day trash and garbage are piled up on a dump. After a while the dump is full. Then a new dump has to be started. People never stop making garbage.

Sometimes a city covers up its old dump. Soil is put on top and grass is planted. There may be a playground or golf course where the dump used to be. Or if the trash is piled high enough, it makes a little mountain. People climb to the top and take pictures of the view.

Garbage and trash don't have to be thrown into dumps. Some things people throw out could be used over and over again. But first they have to be sorted out.

Old bottles and broken glass can be ground up and used to make new glass. Aluminum cans can be melted in big furnaces to make new cans. Good new paper can be made from wastepaper and rags.

You can even use the heat that is made when garbage is burned. Some cities are building special incinerators that are as big as factories. They burn garbage without making dirty smoke. The heat is used to warm stores and offices. It can be used to make electricity. The ashes left in the incinerator can be made into bricks to build new stores and offices.

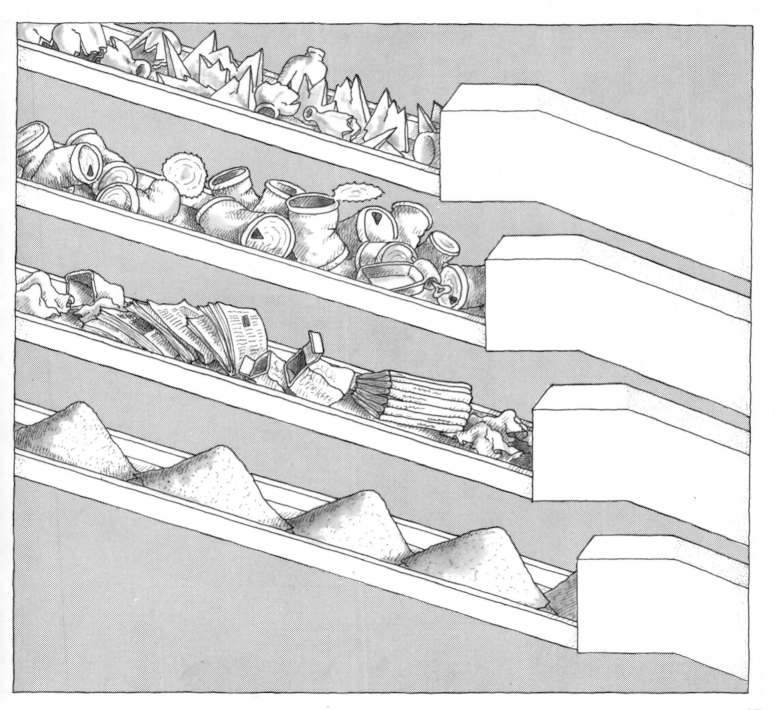

It is not easy to do these things. It costs money to build new incinerators for garbage, and sifters to sort out cans and bottles, and grinders to grind up garbage and glass. But every day people make more and more garbage and trash. They make more than they can get rid of. It keeps piling up.

What do you think we should do about it?

Our teacher asked us this question yesterday. We talked about it. We decided each one of us could help by not making so much trash. When I got home, I fished my old yo-yo out of the garbage pail. It was all gooey. I washed it off. I painted it with some of Mother's enamel. I put in a new string.

Now I have a brand new yo-yo.

ABOUT THE AUTHOR

Paul Showers is a New York newspaperman and writer of nearly two dozen books for children. He first became interested in making books for young readers after watching his own children struggle with the "See, Sally, see" books of the 1950's ("television's greatest boon," he calls them). His own books, most of them in the Let's-Read-and-Find-Out series, have thoroughly proved that children's books can be both lively and worthwhile.

Mr. Showers began newspaper work on the Detroit *Free Press*. Then came the New York *Herald Tribune*, a brief stint on the New York *Sunday Mirror*, and, for the past twenty-seven years, the Sunday *New York Times*. Mr. Showers was born in Sunnyside, Washington, and has an A.B. degree from the University of Michigan.

ABOUT THE ILLUSTRATOR

Loretta Lustig says that she especially enjoyed illustrating this book because she has been concerned with conservation since she was a child. Born in New York City, Ms. Lustig was graduated from Pratt Institute and has worked as an art director for several advertising agencies. This is her first children's book, but she is known to many residents of Manhattan as the geographer of "Dry Dock Country" (a famous series of advertisements). She enjoys reading odd things, making odd things, and collecting odd things, and lives in Brooklyn, which she has found to be the ideal place.